A Thankful HEART

30 Days to the Grateful Life

MITZI NEELY

A Thankful Heart: 30 Days to the Grateful Life

Published by Mitzi Neely, ©2017 Mitzi Neely

Cover Design by: Jana Kennedy-Spicer

CreateSpace Independent Publishing Platform, North Charleston, SC

Printed in the United States of America
First Printing, 2017

ISBN-13: 978-1977541123   ISBN-10:1977541127

To order additional copies of this resource, order online at www.amazon.com or visit www.peacefullyimperfect.net for more information.

Contents

Dedication

None of this would have been possible without God.
He has given me this dream and the support system of
many individuals to make it a reality.

Jerry and Allyson,
thank you for your encouragement and support.
I love you BIG.

Special appreciation to

My mother, Amelia Rowland
My mother-in-law, Lalon Neely Pirkey *(1919-2016)*
In many ways you both shaped who I am today.

My Rah-Rah girls

Robin
Gail
Betsy
Jamie
Dana
Claire
Jennifer
Michelle
Jo Anna
Suzanne
Melanie

Introduction

A Thankful Heart

"Give thanks to the Lord, for He is good, for His steadfast love endures forever."

Psalm 136:1 NIV

This is your invitation to take part in a 30 day challenge leading to the grateful life. Each day is filled with scripture and a short devotional. The study is based on biblical truths to remind us of the importance of gratitude and thankfulness in our everyday lives. Our attitudes, thoughts and actions are at the very core of we are, and this study gives us the opportunity to praise our God daily.

Included in this book is the Daily Scripture Plan, Daily Devotionals, and Journal Pages to keep track of what God is doing in your heart.

As an extra feature and reminder to thank Him for everything, you will find the *'Food for Thought'* section at the end of each week. I have included favorite recipes in honor of the two most influential women in my life: my mother, Amelia Rowland, and my mother-in-law, Lalon Neely Pirkey (1919-2016). I have been blessed to receive the best of what each of these ladies possess.

As you spend time in God's word, meditate on the ways He has blessed you. Take a few moments each day to write down specific thoughts and praises. Thank Him for what He is doing in your life.

While 30 days is a great way to start your 'Thankful Heart' journey, it is my hope that you make it a part of your daily routine to celebrate gratitude and thankfulness every day of the year. There is a lot to be said for cultivating a heart of gratitude that honors God. I'm praying for this experience to bring great joy and growth to your life.

About the Author

Mitzi Neely is an inspiring motivational speaker and writer who encourages women of all ages through her experiences and shortcomings. She has been blessed with a passion and love for people that stretches across the generations.

It is her faith that has motivated her to pursue excellence in all her endeavors. It is Mitzi's primary goal to use her gifts and talents as God leads, always waiting patiently before turning to the right or to the left, listening for His voice saying *"This is the way; walk in it." Isaiah 30:21 NIV*

Her desire whenever she teaches is honesty and transparency, such that God receives glory and honor.

"Whoever speaks on their own does so to gain personal glory, but he who seeks the glory of the one who sent him is a man of truth; there is nothing false about him." John 7:18 NIV

Mitzi's heart is to lighten your load, while conveying the message that nobody's perfect. So often God places certain people in your life at just the right moment; whether the reason is to teach you, grow you in your walk with Him, or to simply love and lift others up. Whatever your struggle or need, you will find encouragement through her words as she refreshes your heart and renews your joy.

Her prayer is that you will find this book encouraging and nourishing.

Mitzi is a wife, mother, and grandmother. She loves sweet tea and hails from the Lone Star State. Aside from her position as a central office administrator in an East Texas school district, she enjoys spending time with her family, writing, speaking, cooking, and sewing.

Follow Mitzi at www.peacefullyimperfect.net because the joy of the journey is learning in His Word together.

30 Day Reading Plan

Day 1 Colossians 3:17; 2 Samuel 22:1-5; 1 Samuel 2:1-10; Ruth 1:12-22

Day 2 Ephesians 1:15-16; Ephesians 5:20; Psalm 107:1, Psalm 9

Day 3 1 Thessalonians 5:18, Matthew 19:26; Philippians 4:13; Proverbs 3:6

Day 4 Psalm 95:1-11; Psalm 47:6

Day 5 Psalm 92:1-15

Day 6 Ezekiel 36:26; 2 Corinthians 5:17; John 3:3

Day 7 James 1:17; Psalm 37:4; Proverbs 15:16-17

Day 8 James 4:10; Jeremiah 17:10; Psalm 34:10

Day 9 2 Corinthians 9:11; Genesis 12:2-3; Proverbs 11:25

Day 10 Psalm 126:3; Isaiah 41:10; James 1:2-4; Philippians 4:19

Day 11 Romans 12:2; 1 Peter 3:3-4; Ephesians 4:22-24; Ephesians 5:8-10

Day 12 1 Timothy 6:6-8; Luke 12:15; Philippians 4:11,19; Hebrews 13:5

Day 13 Psalm 118:24; 1 Peter 5:7; Isaiah 12:4-5

Day 14 3 John 1:2; Romans 12:1; 1 Corinthians 6:19-20

Day 15 Luke 17:15-16; 1 Thessalonians 5:16-18; Romans 8:39

Day 16	Psalm 91:1-2; Jeremiah 29:11; Romans 8:28; Proverbs 3:5
Day 17	Psalm 126:3; Psalm 68:3; Psalm 16:11; Philippians 3:1
Day 18	Psalm 9:1; Psalm 50:23; Colossians 1:3-4
Day 19	Colossians 3:16; 1 Timothy 5:8; 2 Timothy 1:3-5; 3:14-15
Day 20	John 15:12-13; Proverbs 12:26; Colossians 3:12-14; Proverbs 19:20
Day 21	Psalm 107:1-32
Day 22	Lamentations 3:23; James 1:17; John 11:41
Day 23	1 Timothy 4:4; Psalm 9:1; 1 Corinthians 1:4-5
Day 24	Psalm 69:30; Psalm 95:6-7; Psalm 103:20-22; Deuteronomy 8:7-11
Day 25	Philippians 4:11-12; Psalm 106:1; John 10:10 Job 36:11
Day 26	2 Samuel 2:6; 1 Thessalonians 5:18; 1 Chronicles 16:34
Day 27	1 Chronicles 29:12-13; Deuteronomy 6:1-12
Day 28	Psalm 100:4; Psalm 35:18; Psalm 50:14; Psalm 34:1-7
Day 29	Colossians 2:6-7; Ephesians 1:16; 1 Chronicles 23:30
Day 30	2 Corinthians 9:11; Hebrews 13:8; Galatians 1:3; Ephesians 4:6

Prologue
How to be Thankful When God Says No

Over a decade has passed since I thought I was led to prepare for a very specific job. I had received the required certifications, logged hundreds of hours in training, and waited and waited for just the right opportunity.

I developed a focused plan of action to ensure I was ready to apply for that desired position. In fact, all those years ago I laid out every painstaking detail it would take to compete for a position of this caliber. I told God that I had a 10 year time frame to reach this promotion destination, and then time would run out.

God laughed. I didn't hear it at first because I was busy making my own plans and asking Him to bless them.

I was in my twenty-fourth year of teaching when I felt God calling me to step out of the classroom and make the move to school administration. As teachers we call this, 'moving to the dark side.' I didn't really care for the phrase much, but I understood the intent.

So I did it. I moved to the principalship of an elementary campus, and from there to high school principal, to a central administration position, believing along the way that God had placed me right where I needed to be to one day lead a school district.

As I garnered the necessary experiences to be qualified for a top spot, I paid close attention to districts within close proximity with openings, where I would potentially be a good fit. While I was searching for just the place God needed me, I was also fervently praying to not have to move away from my family, my home city, my aging mother, my friends, or my church. I really did believe that God would provide an opportunity close to home, as I was not willing to sacrifice what I had for what I wanted.

So when an opportunity presented itself nearby I took a chance. I had to strongly consider the fact that I had a favorable relationship with the district, but I also knew that I could be affected by baggage that belonged to someone else. There were extraneous things going on behind the scenes that I had no knowledge of, nor any control over.

So I pressed on and weighed the pro's and con's of the position. There was a lot to consider. I thought about not applying but my mind kept saying, 'you'll never know if you don't.' I continued to pray about it and made the decision to go through the paperwork process, submit the application packet and wait.

"For I know the plans I have for you," declares the Lord, "plans to prosper you and not to harm you, plans to give you a hope and a future."
Jeremiah 29:11 NIV

I received a phone call for a first round interview. I was pretty surprised that I had gotten a call at all, but I believed as long as God opened the door I would be willing to walk through it. The first round interview came and went. All pretty general stuff, but there were a few pointed questions that I knew had underlying meanings. I couldn't quite figure out what the interview team was after, but I didn't have a good feeling.

Fast forward to the next week when I received a second call that I was one of the three finalists for the position. Even with my 'not so good feeling,' I remained optimistic. The door was open and I would be obedient and walk through it.

From the moment the first question was asked that night, nothing was as it should have been. The interview team seemed to be very split on what they were looking for. One part of the group was going after the 'baggage' I could not separate from myself. The other part of the team looked as though they were trying to showcase the positive qualities and characteristics I could bring to the table.

What I had hoped would be the start of something meaningful can only be described as outside the scope of what the entire experience should have been.

When I finished the interview that night I left knowing I would not be the candidate of choice. And, then the search firm called a couple of days later to confirm it was not me. I was disappointed of course, as this position was something I had worked for and wanted, but one of the lessons we learn early on in life is that we don't get everything we want.

You see the baggage I referred to earlier—it was someone else's mess that closed this door of opportunity. Why did You let me walk through every single door and not give it to me, I cried out to the Lord?

"The Lord is near to the brokenhearted and saves the crushed in spirit."
Psalm 34:18 ESV

There were a few tears at first, but surprisingly not as many as I had expected. This was a place I thought I had wanted to be. It was about tradition, and family, and in a way, going home. I kept going over and over again how God could have let me walk this journey when He already knew the ending. But, after a few days of replaying the sequence of events and wondering why, I began to see what God wanted me to see through all of this.

It was as if He said, "Mitzi, what were you thinking?"

God knew I didn't go into the experience with blinders on, but I had hoped that the interview team would see my value and know that I would serve them and their community to the best of my ability.

Ultimately though, God had a different plan. He wanted me to see things for what they really were. He wanted me to see the situation I would be in and recognize it was not what I needed. He wanted me to see that the things I believed were important to move forward were not important to the interview team. And, He wanted me to see that things were different and it was no longer home. In the end, nothing I could have said or done would have changed their minds.

At first, I believed I had failed. I had not achieved this particular goal on my career list. I had been working on this for over a decade and it was the final checkbox for getting everything I had ever wanted. What could I have done differently?

Honestly, there wasn't anything that could have been done. You see, that is how the enemy misleads us to believe his lies. He plants seeds of doubt. He wants us to believe that circumstances, failures, and successes define us. He wants us to believe that we have been ripped off, short changed, and wronged.

None of that is truth.

We are defined by our Maker and Creator. It is about who we are. It is about how well we hold up in the midst of adversity. It is about how well we deal with disappointments, big and small, and it is about how well we rebound and see God's hand of protection in all that we do.

> *"May the beloved of the Lord dwell in security by Him,*
> *"Who shields him all the day,*
> *And he dwells between His shoulders."*
> *Deuteronomy 33:12 NASB*

There is no doubt that I could have let a grudge take root in my heart. It is our humanness that allows us to slip off into the brink of unforgiveness. It would have been easy to do, but I knew I was better than that. I am a 'Daughter of the King,' who is bigger than any issue, challenge, problem, person, or situation. And I am most thankful that He sees the big picture and knows what is best for me, even when I don't see it or understand.

> *"My thoughts are nothing like your thoughts," says the Lord.*
> *"And my ways are far beyond anything you could imagine.*
> *For just as the heavens are higher than the earth,*
> *so my ways are higher than your ways*
> *and my thoughts higher than your thoughts."*
> *Isaiah 55:8-9 NLT*

I could have become discouraged and lost my way. I could have hung my head in shame believing I had failed. Or, I could have made the decision not to pursue this opportunity.

But what would I have gained from believing these mistruths?

Instead, God's use of this situation breathed new life in me and a totally different plan and direction. I had so much to be thankful and grateful for. In the midst of the disappointment I realized I was already doing exactly what I needed to do and, surprisingly what I found I really wanted to do. And I had to remember that while things did not go the way I had planned, they did go the way I had prayed.

You see, I had put this work, God's call to ministry, in a 'drawer' to focus on what I thought He was calling me to do professionally.

Instead, He was preparing me to pursue my call and love of Him more passionately and deeply.

God's wild pursuit down this path had a completely different destination than I expected.

And here it is. With you.

And, I am beyond grateful.

Day 1
Cultivate Gratitude

"And whatever you do, whether in word or deed, do it all in the name of the Lord Jesus, giving thanks to God the Father through Him."

Colossians 3:17 NIV

There are numerous examples of men and women in scripture who, regardless of their circumstances, thanked God for what He did in their lives.

Ruth was willing to give up her life as she knew it and stay with her mother-in-law Naomi because she trusted God. Hannah prayed fervently for a child. She didn't know if that glorious day would ever come, but she had faith. God plucked David from the field tending His sheep and made him a King. But first, he had to slay a giant.

None of these situations were without challenges or mistakes. But each person followed the Lord and honored His will for their life.

Each one of these individuals experienced tremendous changes and uncertainty, but they continued to look to God and seek His truths.

Talk about a group of people who were filled with uncertainty, fear, and anxiety. And yet in the midst of everything, they were grateful and thankful.

Ask the Lord to cultivate in you a more grateful heart. If you have realized that your thankful heart is less than it should be, pray about your shortcomings. Ask Him to forgive you and to change your heart and soul into a truly thankful individual.

Point of Focus

"Regardless of the challenges faced or mistakes made, we can count on God to see us through any situation."

Scripture Reading

2 Samuel 22:1-5

_____

_____

_____

1 Samuel 2:1-10

_____

_____

_____

Ruth 1:12-22

_____

_____

_____

Are you in a place right now that makes it hard to thank God on a consistent basis? Lay your burdens at His feet and pray for guidance and wisdom.

Today, I am thankful for

_____

_____

Prayer

Lord, I want to praise Your name always—even when things get hard.
Please help me to remember to thank You for every situation I face today.
You see the big picture and know what is best for my life and I am
exceedingly grateful for You. In Your Name, Amen.

Day 2

Thankful Heart

"I have not stopped giving thanks for you, remembering you in my prayers."

Ephesians 1:16 NIV

King David is a man known for praise. Even during the darkest of seasons, he always pointed back to the goodness of God. Scripture says David whistled, laughed, and jumped for joy. He sang with a great spirit to the LORD when He delivered him from the hand of all his enemies and from the hand of Saul. God made a covenant promise to David, and what did he do? David prayed a prayer of thanks.

Regardless of the challenges and mistakes he made, David responded with a thankful heart to God.

It's not always easy to be thankful in the midst of adversity or trial. Yet David models time and time again what it means to have a heart of gratitude.

Read through the passages below and ask God to reveal your thankful heart. Reflect on what you've read and praise Him for your blessings.

Point of Focus

"Regardless of how today unfolds for me Lord, I want to walk confidently in Your promises and praise You for the blessings You have given me."

Scripture Reading

Ephesians 1:15-16

_____

_____

_____

Ephesians 5:20

_____

_____

_____

Psalm 107:1

_____

_____

_____

Psalm 9

_____

_____

_____

What do these scriptures reveal to you about gratitude?

_____

_____

Today, I am thankful for

_____

_____

Prayer

Father God, I come to you today with a grateful heart. I praise your name and rejoice in all things good about my life. Even when I am faced with challenges, I know You are with me. Thank you for everything You have done, and continue to do for me. In Your name I pray, Amen.

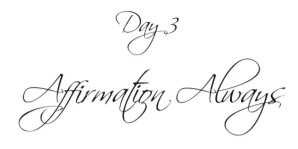

Day 3

Affirmation Always

"Give thanks in all circumstances, for this is God's will for you in Christ Jesus."

1 Thessalonians 5:18 NIV

Paul is the author of 1 Thessalonians. He begins this letter with a note of affirmation, thanking God for the strong faith and good reputation of the Thessalonians. He reminds us that his teachings were not about 'thanking God for everything,' but *'in everything.'*

I am so thankful and appreciative when friends come to my rescue. There are times when I find myself immersed in a busy season of life and become overwhelmed. Over and over again, my closest friends will say, "What can we do for you? How can we pray for you?" Those are sweet words to my soul.

Think about some of the tough times in your life. How has God worked in you and what are you thankful for as a result? We often show our appreciation and love to others through words of affirmation and encouragement. Do you do the same when you pray to God?

Point of Focus

"Make it a habit to thank people for their kindness. God provides for us any time, day or night, and often through answered prayer."

Scripture Reading

Matthew 19:26

_____

_____

_____

Philippians 4:13

_____

_____

_____

Proverbs 3:6

_____

_____

_____

Today, I am thankful for

_____

_____

Prayer

Dear Lord, thank you for those individuals who are willing to help me when I am in need. I pray that I can provide the same love and kindness to each one, and shower them with buckets of gratitude. Amen.

Sing Praises to Him

"Come let us sing for joy to the Lord; let us shout aloud to the Rock of our salvation. Let us come before Him with thanksgiving and extol Him with music and song."

Psalm 95:1-2 NIV

This Psalm is an invitation to worship God. We are to sing to the Lord and shout aloud. Sounds like a joyful celebration doesn't it? Of course singing is not the only way to honor and worship our God, but it is an important way.

I love to honor my God with a happy heart—one of enthusiasm. And despite the setbacks or challenges that I may deal with on a daily basis, I have much to celebrate joyfully about. God wants us to come before Him with thanksgiving. I am reminded of one of my favorite choruses, 'I will enter His gates with thanksgiving in my heart. I will enter His courts with praise.'

If we are to receive His ultimate blessings then we must not lose faith, let our hearts harden, or become ensnared in our stubbornness. We are to praise God at every turn and worship Him with grateful hearts.

Point of Focus

"Honor and celebrate God with a happy heart, shouting aloud and joyfully. We are to come to Him with thanksgiving. "

Scripture Reading

Psalm 95:1-11

_____

_____

_____

Psalm 47:6

_____

_____

_____

What are your favorite ways to praise the Lord? Make a list of your 5 favorite praise & worship songs and listen to them during the month.

List Your Favorite Ways to Praise the Lord

_____

_____

_____

5 Favorite Praise & Worship Songs

_____

_____

_____

Today, I am thankful for

_____

_____

Prayer

Father God, I come to you today with thanksgiving and gratitude. Help me to focus my heart and mind on You and Your Word. I love that You delight in me and that you rejoice over me with singing. I will praise you Lord, with all my heart; I will glorify your name forever. In Your Holy Name. Amen.

Day 5

An Attitude of Gratitude

*"It is good to praise the Lord and make music to Your name.
O Most High, proclaiming Your love in the morning
and Your faithfulness at night."*

Psalm 92:1-2 NIV

This Psalm is about being thankful and faithful every day. The holiday season tends to be the time we pause and give thanks daily to God. But in reality, every season should be about giving thanks to Him.

We can all take a few minutes each day to focus on our blessings, but genuine thanks should be on our lips continuously.

My prayer time may vary from place to place, but what I want most from my time with God is to honor Him with praise and thanksgiving. The thankfulness that flows from my mouth is sincere and heartfelt.

Before I lay out my prayer requests each day, I praise Him with something I am thankful for; something straight from my heart. I don't want every prayer to be me asking for something. I want to come into His presence to thank Him for the love and grace He extends to me daily. I want to remember that even in the midst of uncertainty I see His Light shining through. He wraps me in His protection and is gracious with His provision. Things may not always work out as I have prayed, but they do work out according to His Will and what is best for my life.

Point of Focus

"An attitude of gratitude will carry me through life's most difficult storms."

Scripture Reading

Psalm 92:1-15

What does this Psalm teach us about attitude and gratitude? How can we honor God on a daily basis? Do you give God the first five minutes of your day?

_____

_____

_____

_____

_____

_____

Today, I am thankful for

_____

_____

Prayer

Gracious Heavenly Father, I bow before You today and lay my difficulties and negative thoughts at Your feet. Please help me to adopt an attitude of gratitude no matter what circumstances I face. I trust You and I love You. In Jesus Name, Amen.

Day 6

A Day of Transformation

"Moreover, I will give you a new heart and put a new spirit within you; and I will remove the heart of stone from your flesh and give you a heart of flesh."

Ezekiel 36:26 NIV

In the Old Testament God promised to restore Israel. He gave them a new heart for following Him and put His spirit within them, transforming them and empowering them to do His will.

His powerful love endures forever and even in the midst of changing circumstances, transformation takes place. We see it over and over again throughout the Bible.

In John 4, another transformation occurred. This time though, it was during an impromptu meeting between Jesus and the woman at the well.

One day while Jesus and the disciples were traveling through Samaria, He encountered a woman who had gone to the well during the heat of the day. Maybe she was there to avoid gossip from others, but her meeting with Jesus was not a chance encounter. Timing was everything. During their visit she told Jesus her spiritual beliefs and that she knew of the Messiah. Right then and there, Jesus told her He was the Messiah and the water He offered would satisfy all thirstiness; Jesus was telling her that He is the giver of eternal life.

From that day forward, the Samaritan woman was transformed. Her attitude changed; she had new standing in the community, and her beliefs changed. How did it happen? From a perfectly timed face-to-face encounter with Jesus.

Point of Focus

"No matter what has happened in your life, God offers you a fresh start."

Write a brief story of transformation. What changed in your life and have you shared the good news with others?

_____

_____

_____

_____

_____

Scripture Reading

2 Corinthians 5:17

_____

_____

_____

John 3:3

_____

_____

_____

Today, I am thankful for

Prayer

Most gracious Heavenly Father, hear my prayers. I come to You today, believing in You and Your promises. I lay my sins at your feet and pray for a new beginning. Thank you for giving me chance after chance to turn over a new leaf and start fresh. From the moment I asked you into my heart, You transformed me to see as You see and to be more like You. I pray these things in your most precious and Holy Name. Amen.

Day 7

Blessings Big & Small

"Every good and perfect gift is from above, coming down from the Father of the heavenly lights, who does not change like shifting shadows."

James 1:17 NIV

Notice the word '*every*' in James 1:17. Every good and perfect gift is from God. I am so thankful for His abundant provision. As a teenager I was impressed by the tangible gifts I was given. Now, as I find myself on the older side of things, I am more thankful than ever for my family, my home, the love I receive, and the blessed assurance I have as a Christian.

James wrote these words as a reminder of the greatest gift of all—our Lord and Savior. The spiritual gifts alone keep me in awe. He is the Light of the World. There is no gift that out weighs or gives more than Christ.

We have so much to be thankful for. That includes the big and the little. Are there blessings that God has provided, big or small, that you haven't thanked Him for?

Take the time right now to bow your head and pray a prayer of thanksgiving to Him. Jot down a few of His blessings and record in the journal space below.

_____

_____

_____

_____

Point of Focus

"The best gifts and blessings in life, big or small, come from God."

Scripture Reading

Psalm 37:4

Proverbs 15:16-17

Today, I am thankful for

Prayer

Heavenly Father I am so blessed by the gifts You have given me. Create in me a grateful heart that looks forward to praising You in every moment. Show me who You are and open my eyes to reveal Your goodness, grace, and love that endures forever. Amen.

Food for Thought

Heavenly Father,

Thank you for blessing us with this day.
May we be a shining light to those who are gathered around this table. Thank you for the food that we are about to eat; may it nourish our bodies. Amen.

Party Potatoes

Kim Dobson gave me this recipe about 25 years ago when our church was planning to serve dinner after a Christmas Choir Cantata. I have prepared this dish too many times to count over the years and it is a requested favorite by family and friends.

This recipe is super delicious and subject to rave reviews. This is my go-to dish for church suppers, family dinners, and it has accompanied numerous meat dishes for families/individuals who need a meal during an illness.

It's easy, bakes in one dish, and there's no need to feel bad about the calories. Just enjoy.

Ingredients

1 bag southern style hash browns (little cubes—not shredded)
1 pint whipping cream
2-3 cups grated cheese
Salt and pepper
Parsley flakes
1 1/2 sticks margarine, melted

Directions

1. Preheat oven to 375 degrees.
2. Using a 9x13 casserole dish lightly spray cooking spray on bottom and sides of dish.
3. Place potatoes in dish and salt and pepper.
4. Pour whipping cream over potatoes, add grated cheese, and sprinkle parsley over the cheese. Pour melted butter over cheese.
5. Cover with foil and bake 50 minutes covered; cook uncovered for another 30-40 minutes until lightly brown.

Serves 8-10

Poppyseed Chicken

Thankfully I married into a family where good food and good cooks are plentiful. My sister-in-law, Donna Reeves, is a wonderful cook and she shared this recipe with me over two decades ago. It has been a staple in our home ever since. It is an often requested dish and my daughter continues the tradition today, preparing it for her own family. This was also one of my mother-in-law's favorite dishes. It's a great comfort food, easy to prepare and can be made ahead of time.

Ingredients

2 chicken breasts, cooked/chopped or 2-3 cups of rotisserie chicken
1 - 8 oz. cream cheese
2 cans of Cream of Chicken soup; I use low fat.
1 1/2 sleeves of Ritz Crackers (sleeves are the rolls of crackers)
2 Tbsp. poppy seed
Salt and pepper
1 1/2 sticks margarine, melted

Directions

1. Preheat oven to 350 degrees.
2. Lightly coat bottom and sides of a 9x13 dish with cooking spray.
3. Place chopped/cooked chicken in dish; sprinkle with salt and pepper.
4. In a heavy duty sauce pan stir cream cheese and soups until smooth. Continue to stir so mixture doesn't scorch.
5. Pour soup mixture over chicken.
6. Place crackers into a gallon ziploc bag and use a rolling pin to crush until fine.
7. Mix poppy seeds in with crackers and shake bag until poppy seeds are evenly distributed.
8. Sprinkle cracker mixture over cream cheese mixture.
9. Melt margarine and pour over top of cracker mixture and bake for 40 minutes until bubbly. Serves: 6-8

Day 8
Guard Against Entitlement

"Humble yourselves before the Lord, and He will exalt you."

James 4:10 ESV

It's easy to be happy and thankful when our hearts overflow with gratitude because of the good things going on in our lives. But sometimes it is those full hearts that lead us to feel entitled and become entangled in the 'it's all about me,' syndrome.

I don't want entitlement to become a habit or a way of life; that kind of thinking is worldly and it is dangerous. I want to honor God with my thoughts and my actions.

Those who are committed to the Lord don't spend much time thinking about themselves or about what they don't have. It's about feeling grateful for what they do have.

List and describe two things that you have felt entitled to in recent days. Then humbly bow your head and confess your prideful ways and ask for His continued blessings upon you.

_____

_____

_____

_____

_____

Point of Focus

"I am entitled to nothing, but God has blessed me with everything."

Scripture Reading

Jeremiah 17:10

_____

_____

_____

Psalm 34:10

_____

_____

_____

Today, I am thankful for

_____

_____

Prayer

Father, I come to you with a heart of gratitude. I pray that I never fall into the trap of entitlement and discontent. Protect me from becoming prideful and using my human ways to gain what I do not deserve. In your precious Name, Amen.

Day 9

Giving & Generosity

You will be made rich in every way so that you can be generous on every occasion, and through us your generosity will result in thanksgiving to God.

2 Corinthians 9:11 NIV

Where gratitude grows, so should generosity. When you feel deep gratitude you often want to help others who are in need. Every day is the season for giving as we are met with requests from community agencies, programs, and special projects.

Pray for wisdom and discernment as you make decisions to help others. Determine if you want to spend time with people in need, give your talents to a special project, or give financially to a cause you are passionate about. Whatever it is, do it.

God's word says that we are to be a grateful people who are generous. Acts 20:35 reminds us that "it is more blessed to give than to receive."

Point of Focus

"We are to be a generous and giving body of believers."

Scripture Reading

Genesis 12:2-3

_____

_____

_____

Proverbs 11:25

_____

_____

_____

Today I am thankful for

_____

_____

Prayer

Father, I come to You today to thank you for Your generosity and gift of eternal life. You are the giver of all good and perfect gifts and I praise You for my attitude of gratitude and generosity. Help me to honor You through my giving heart. Amen.

Day 10

Count Your Blessings One by One

"The Lord has done great things for us, and we are filled with joy."

Psalm 126:3 NIV

There are so many ways to count your blessings. You can journal about your blessings, create quotes and scriptures to memorize or carry with you, or teach your children about gratitude and thankfulness through activities and bible lessons.

I taught my grand girls to keep track of their praises and blessings in a *Gratitude* jar. Of course they each made one during our 'Camp Nana,' time a couple of summers ago and we found it is the perfect way to document their daily blessings, surprise moments, LOL moments, favorite memories with family/friends and special accomplishments.

I encourage them to empty the jar twice during the year and re-read the things they were grateful for. I want them to be reminded of God's faithfulness over and over again. Think about the blessings you could place in your *Gratitude* jar.

Point of Focus

"Make note of your praises and blessings and be reminded of God's faithfulness throughout the year."

Scripture Reading

Isaiah 41:10

_____

_____

_____

James 1:2-4

_____

_____

_____

Philippians 4:19

_____

_____

_____

Today, I am thankful for

_____

_____

Prayer

Dear Lord, thank You for my daily blessings. My heart overflows with the joy, love, and goodness You shower on me daily. Keep my eyes focused on You and help me to remember all that You do *in* me. Thank you for the memories You make in my day-to-day life. I pray that I count each one by name. In your Precious Name, Amen.

For more information and instructions on creating a Gratitude Jar, check out: http://peacefullyimperfect.net/thankful-for-the-blessings-and-time-together/

Day 11

Let the Real You Shine Through

"Do not be conformed to this world, but be transformed by the renewal of your mind, that by testing you may discern what is the will of God, what is good and acceptable and perfect."

Romans 12:2 ESV

In a world where we are saturated with people who are self-centered, mean-spirited or show little respect for others, it's easy to become tired and worn down from the negativity.

Instead we must surround ourselves with positivity and uplifting words and actions. We are to model kindness, gentleness, harmony and peace. We must respond with the 'Golden Rule' and treat others as we would want to be treated.

Our goal is to live a life of gratitude and thankfulness. If we are intentional and genuine with our commitment to Christ, we can change the world. We can use our servant hearts along with acts of gratitude and kindness to be *GAME CHANGERS*.

List two ways you can make a difference to others. Living by the fruit of the Spirit will astonish the messed up world you live in.

_____

_____

_____

_____

Point of Focus

"A thankful heart can make a positive difference in a negative atmosphere."

Scripture Reading

1 Peter 3:3-4

_____

_____

_____

Ephesians 4:22-24

_____

_____

_____

Ephesians 5:8-10

_____

_____

_____

Today, I am thankful for

Prayer

Lord, I come today seeking You and Your promises. I pray Your hedge of protection over me as I walk through this life sharing Your word with others. May I be intentional with all You have blessed me with as I look for ways to spread light over this dark world. Amen.

Day 12
Think, 'Less is More'

"But Godliness with contentment is great gain, for we brought nothing into the world, and we cannot take anything out of the world.
But if we have food and clothing, with these will be content."

1 Timothy 6:6-8 ESV

Contentment is the greatest form of wealth. But in a society that breeds discontent and greed, it is easy to get caught up in wanting more in order to be happy.

There have been times, particularly in my younger years that I became ensnared in what the world offered and I wanted more than I deserved. The longing for more fuels the desire for bigger stuff, more money, and often times, the accumulation of debt that goes with it.

I know this is not what my Father wants. What He wants me to see is that He has blessed me over and over again with all the possessions I need, the love and support of faithful family and friends, and the contentment of living freely, without the heavy weight of burdens.

During your prayer time this week let God know you are not asking for anything, but instead thanking Him for all you have. Happiness isn't getting all you want. It's enjoying all you have.

Point of Focus

"Happiness is enjoying what I have; not getting what I want."

Luke 12:15

_____

_____

_____

Philippians 4:11,19

_____

_____

_____

Hebrews 13:5

_____

_____

_____

Today I am thankful for

_____

_____

Prayer

Father in Heaven, I come to You today laying all of my selfish desires at Your feet. I am so thankful for Your unconditional love and forgiveness when I mess up. You pick me up when I fall down, and You stand by me, holding my hand when I'm afraid to take the next step. There's nothing perfect about me but I can pray for my actions to be Christ-like. I love You Lord and I seek to honor You daily. In Your precious name, I pray. Amen.

Day 13

When You're Not Feeling Grateful

"This is the day which the Lord has made; we will rejoice and be glad in it."

Psalm 118:24 NKJV

There are days I wake up and just can't seem to get moving. Oh, I am totally thankful for the opportunity to have another day, but occasionally I'm a slow starter—sluggish and out of sync. It seems as though very little of the juices, creative or otherwise, are pumping inside of me.

If truth be told, it would be easy to wallow in the miry muck and clay of negativity, but I know I can't. That is not what God wants from me. Instead I choose to put a smile on my face, strap on the armor of God, remember who I belong to, and conjure up a little gratitude.

With His words planted firmly in my heart I know I can make the decision to be grateful for all parts of my life. And the steps I take to follow through on this decision will require continuous prayer along with asking God to cultivate in me a heart of gratitude. I must trust Him even through the challenging times and circumstances, for there is nothing too big for God to handle.

Think about those times when you are not at your best. God wants you to give your burdens over to Him and ask Him to breathe new life into you. That's what I do.

Point of Focus

"Consistently practicing gratitude gives our life meaning and it allows us to experience the rich blessings God has in store for us."

Scripture Reading

1 Peter 5:7

_____

_____

_____

Isaiah 12:4-5

_____

_____

_____

Today, I am thankful for

_____

_____

Prayer

Dear Lord, I praise Your name. Please direct my steps as I arise this morning and be with me as I go throughout this day. Forgive me for procrastinating and looking for the easy way out; instead help me to use the talents and abilities You have given me to handle anything. Strengthen my heart and renew my joy as only You can do. In Your name I pray. Amen.

Day 14
Reap the Benefits of a Thankful Heart

"Dear friend, I pray that you may enjoy good health and that all may go well with you, even as your soul is getting along well."

3 John 1:2 NIV

A heart full of gratitude does the body good and contributes to spiritual health. It's important to enjoy a continuous season of thankfulness. Don't let stress overwhelm you. Every day presents new opportunities, so take advantage of each one.

Be intentional with your time and focus on what matters to you. Refrain from keeping an endless to-do list. Plan for some quiet time to meditate and reflect on Scripture that brings you comfort.

Make a point to power down an evening or two a week to spend uninterrupted time with your family—everyone deserves to unplug from all the busyness around us, and it is good for the soul.

Remember an attitude of gratitude contributes to your well-being.

Point of Focus

"A thankful heart yields a happier life."

Scripture Reading

Romans 12:1

_____

_____

_____

1 Corinthians 6:19-20

_____

_____

_____

Today, I am thankful for

_____

_____

Prayer

Dear Lord, Thank you for your unconditional love and the abundance of blessings that are far more than I deserve. Continue to show me day after day how gratitude benefits my physical health, my emotional health and my spiritual heart. Father, you are the source of my joy and happiness and I pray that you will continue to cover me in your grace, goodness and mercy. In your precious name, Amen.

Food for Thought

Dear Lord,

I come praising Your wonderful name for the meal we are about to enjoy. Thank you for this time together as a family and I pray for your guidance in our conversations and fellowship. In Your name we pray. Amen.

Two, Two, Easy Peach Cobbler

This wonderful dessert is a favorite all year long. Typically we think of peaches in the summertime, but thanks to my mother-in-law, Lalon Neely Pirkey, I keep peaches in the freezer year round. I've included the bonus recipe on the next page for preparing fresh peaches for the freezer. Several of my friends have also made this dessert with fresh plums and blackberries.

I love to prepare this cobbler in a cast iron skillet; but it can be prepared in a 9x13 casserole dish.

Ingredients

1 (29 oz) can Peaches or 3 cups *fresh peaches
2 sticks butter or margarine, melted
2 cups sugar
2 cups flour
2 cups milk
2 teaspoons baking powder

Directions

1. Preheat oven to 350 degrees. Lightly grease baking dish or cast iron skillet.
2. Pour drained can of peaches or 3 cups of *fresh peaches into 12 inch cast iron skillet or 9x13 baking dish. Pour melted butter over the peaches.
3. In a bowl, mix sugar, flour, milk, and baking powder to form a batter. Pour batter over peaches and butter.
4. Bake for 30-45 minutes until top is golden brown and edges are crispy. The recipe will take 45-55 minutes in the cast iron skillet.

Serves: 8

Best Frozen Peaches

Here's the recipe I use with fresh peaches so I have a supply in the freezer for several months. My precious mother-in-law shared this with me years ago and it gives the peaches a wonderful flavor that is preserved even after they are frozen.

8-9 cups peeled, sliced peaches

1 Tablespoon lemon juice

1 cup sugar

3 teaspoons fruit fresh

1/2 cup orange juice.

In a large bowl mix peaches and lemon juice; in a separate bowl mix sugar and fruit fresh. Then toss peaches with sugar mixture. Pour orange juice over layers and refrigerate 2-3 hours. Then divide into equal amounts into quart size ziploc freezer bags, or seal with your seal saver and freeze.

Understanding Gratitude

"One of them, when he saw he was healed, came back, praising God in a loud voice. He threw himself at Jesus' feet and thanked Him--and he was a Samaritan."

Luke 17:15-16 NIV

For some people expressing gratitude isn't a priority, especially if it's not practiced daily. A quote by Meister Eckhart says,

"If the only prayer you say in your life is 'thank you,' that would suffice."

Making the effort to express gratitude is huge. But we must have an understanding of why it's important. Grateful Christians grow in God's grace and while He does not demand that we thank Him, He is pleased when we do so.

The story of the ten lepers in Luke 17 speaks volumes about those who realize they should be grateful and thankful. Only one of the ten lepers returned to thank Jesus for his healing, while the others may have taken the healing for granted. Jesus even asked the one who returned where the other nine were. He said, "Was no one found to return and give praise to God except this foreigner? Then He said to him, 'Rise and go; your faith has made you well."

Point of Focus

"Expressing gratitude enables me to glorify God and grow in His grace."

Scripture Reading

1 Thessalonians 5:16-18

_____

_____

_____

Romans 8:39

_____

_____

_____

How do you make time to thank God for the blessings He provides?
Describe a recent experience that prompted you to thank God.

_____

_____

_____

Today, I am thankful for

_____

_____

Prayer

Father God, help me to express my gratitude at every turn. Everything I have and everything I am is because of You. I want to thank You for seeing the big picture and taking care of me even when I do not understand. Help me to remember to thank and appreciate the actions of others through kind words and a kind heart. In Your name I pray. Amen.

Day 16
Use All Things For Good

*"He who dwells in the shelter of the Most High will rest in the shadow of the Almighty. I will say of the Lord,
He is my refuge and my fortress, my God, in whom I trust. "*

Psalm 91:1-2 NIV

Life's challenges are often more than we want to deal with. Everyone experiences ups and downs, major and minor setbacks, and disappointments.

It's through these times we pray for God's will, His protection, and His grace. We pray for His peace and strength to sustain us and to help us realize as we hold on to our faith that He has a perfect plan for us; a plan that is far superior to anything that we can conjure up on our own.

Write this statement in your journal as an encouragement to pursuing a grateful heart. 'Cultivate the habit of being grateful for everything that comes to you--good or bad, there is a lesson to be learned.'

If we say we are fully committed to Christ then we must trust Him completely in every decision and choice that we make.

Point of Focus

"There will be challenges in life, but God sustains and extends His grace and mercy to us each and every time."

Scripture Reading

Jeremiah 29:11

Romans 8:28

Proverbs 3:5

Today, I am thankful for

Prayer

Jesus, I thank You for extending Your grace and encouragement to me in times of trial. Each time I bump into trouble it is through You and Your character building moments that I can find my way clearly through a situation. Thank you for Your perfect plan and for steering me in the direction I should go. Amen.

Finding Your Joy is the Ticket

"The Lord has done great things for us, and we are filled with joy."

Psalm 126:3 NIV

God's word commands us to 'Rejoice in the Lord.' We are to be joyful always and realize that our joy is for His glory. The word 'joy' appears in the Bible anywhere from 58 to 160 times depending on the translation. Joy comes through persevering through the trials and challenges and leaning on Christ as our faith grows and strengthens. In other words, the joy we feel and experience is the deep, abiding kind that is long-lasting.

So be the joy for those around you. Be a light for Him as you choose to be obedient and follow Him. Real joy comes through transforming your heart and attitude into one of gratitude.

Point of Focus

"The joy we feel through Christ is the deep, abiding kind that draws us to Him."

Scripture Reading

Psalm 68:3

_____

_____

_____

Psalm 16:11

_____

_____

_____

Philippians 3:1

_____

_____

_____

Today, I am thankful for

_____

_____

Prayer

Dear Lord, I want to rejoice in You always. Help me to be a light for others as my cup overflows with Your abundance and good news. Let me find unending joy as I spend time in Your Word and draw closer to You. Amen.

Day 18

Gratitude Sets Us Free

"I will give thanks to You, LORD, with all my heart;
I will tell of all Your wonderful deeds."

Psalm 9:1 NIV

We are to be thankful in all things. You see God doesn't owe us--we are the ones with the debt. Often times our choices create situations that do not benefit us and lead us down the road of discontent where we want more, buy more, and feel like we deserve more.

As we travel this journey of faithfulness and obedience we ought to be compelled to look for freedom from all of the worldly goods. We should be grateful for our family, our friends, our marriage and spouse, our kids, our home and our job. Our lives will not be perfect, but the blessings far outweigh the negatives. The more we pray for God to cultivate in us a grateful heart, the better off we are spiritually, emotionally, mentally and physically.

We can be thankful to God for all the things that have gone right and grateful that we are no longer bogged down in the pit. It is time to let gratitude be our path to freedom.

Point of Focus

"Gratitude guards my heart from focusing on worldly gain."

Scripture Reading

Psalm 50:23

_____

_____

_____

Colossians 1:3-4

_____

_____

_____

Describe how you worked through a challenging experience or situation, and what you learned through your journey.

_____

_____

_____

Today, I am thankful for

_____

_____

Prayer

Dear Heavenly Father, please let my heart of gratitude honor You and draw others closer to You. You are the reason and source of all that I have and all that I am. I want my attitude of gratitude to be contagious and a light for your Kingdom. I praise Your Holy name day in and day out and I dedicate this season of thanksgiving to the King of Kings, giving You praise, glory and honor. Amen!

Day 19
Grateful Is As Grateful Does

"Let the word of Christ dwell in you richly, teaching and admonishing one another in all wisdom, singing psalms and hymns and spiritual songs, with thankfulness in your hearts to God."

Colossians 3:16 ESV

Be a model of gratitude. It is so important for us to tell our family and friends how much we appreciate them. We won't always agree on every subject. We won't always understand what makes the other tick, but we all possess unique abilities, talents and skills. In other words, we ALL have something worthwhile to contribute.

As parents or guardians, we are tasked with building character in our children. With that responsibility comes teaching manners, kindness, and integrity. We must model the behaviors we want our kids to carry throughout their lives. Let them see you tell your spouse how much he or she means to you and how thankful you are to have them in your life. Let them see you care for others in need. Volunteer as a family in a community event or seasonal project. Lead by example.

Make the practice of gratitude a habit. Emphasize how important 'thank you' is. Encourage acts of kindness. Tend to those in need.

Simply put, tell your family how grateful you are for them. Tell them you appreciate their presence. Model gratitude and thankfulness at home. Family is your legacy.

"Make the practice of gratitude a part of your every day life
and tell others how much they mean to you."

Scripture Reading

1 Timothy 5:8

_____

_____

_____

2 Timothy 1:3-5

_____

_____

_____

2 Timothy 3:14-15

_____

_____

_____

How do you tell your family you are thankful for them? Record your answer
below. Make it a priority right now.

_____

_____

_____

_____

_____

Today, I am thankful for

_____

_____

Prayer

Father God, I come to You today thanking You for the gift of family and friends. We may not always see eye to eye, but we are children of the King. We all possess different talents and abilities, but through respect and appreciation we can help others feel valued. Help us hold each other close and model the behavior You so desire in us. Amen.

Day 20

Thankful for Friends

"This is my commandment, that you love one another as I have loved you. Greater love has no one than this, that someone lay down his life for his friends."

John 15:12-13 ESV

Our FRIENDS make up such a huge part of our lives that in many instances we consider them to be more like family. It's wise to have an assortment of friends who span the generations because they bring diversity, appreciation, wisdom, perspective and love.

God's word tells us in Proverbs 13:20 to choose our friends wisely. True friends make up our inner circle. We appreciate them, love them and count on them. When I think of the qualities that are important in a friend, I value people who are loyal, sincere, loving , supportive, giving, honest, dependable, and trustworthy. It is those same qualities that I must possess as a friend.

There is great comfort knowing that a good friend loves at all times.

My hope is that you are united with a group of friends who are grounded in faith and followers of Jesus Christ. Your friendships should represent who He is and what He's done through each of us. It doesn't get any better than that.

Point of Focus

"A friendship that reflects Christ's character is a gift from God."

Scripture Reading

Proverbs 12:26

_____

_____

_____

Colossians 3:12-14

_____

_____

_____

Proverbs 19:20

_____

_____

_____

Make a list of the special friends in your life and describe why they mean so much to you. Write each of them a note expressing your thankfulness. There will be blessings all around.

_____

_____

_____

_____

Today, I'm thankful for

_____

_____

Prayer

Heavenly Father, I feel so privileged to have the opportunity to love others as You have loved me. Family and friends are gifts from You to us and there is great comfort knowing I am surrounded by special individuals You have put in my path. May I continue to seek out those friends who are grounded in faith and follow You. Thank you for your abundance and unconditional love, and for creating special relationships along the way. Amen.

Day 21
Tell Your Story

"Give thanks to the Lord, for He is good; His love endures forever."

Psalm 107:1 NIV

This chapter of the Psalms is one of forty-three that applauds God's works, describes the blessings and benefits of virtuous living, thanks God for His mercy, and praises Him for His wonderful Word. Living a faithful and obedient life is the best gift we can give to God.

We are reminded of God's great love for His people as four different 'testimonies' are shared in this chapter. Regardless of the situation or crisis, His Word shows those who have been redeemed by the Lord and who have reason to thank Him.

In these four situations there is a common thread connecting each one. Each shows distress, desperation, and deliverance—each time ending with the thanksgiving chorus, 'Let them give thanks to the Lord for His unfailing love and His wonderful deeds for men.'

As we look at our own lives do we see that same common thread? How many times have we found ourselves in distress, cried out to Him, and ask Him to deliver us?

Point of Focus

"God's love never fails; therefore, I can thank Him in every circumstance."

Scripture Reading

Psalm 107:1-32

Think about YOUR STORY. Do you see similarities between your story and these verses? Describe how God redeemed you and what differences you see in your life today. Tell what Christ has done for you and in you.

_____

_____

_____

_____

_____

_____

_____

Today, I am thankful for

_____

_____

Prayer

Dear Heavenly Father, thank you for redeeming me and for all that You have done in my life. I am so grateful You know my distresses, hear my cries and lovingly provide me with deliverance. Regardless of my situation You are always doing more than I can ever see or think possible. Because of You Lord I am surrounded by an abundance of blessings big and small. I trust You and I love You Lord. Amen.

Food for Thought

Our Most Gracious Heavenly Father,

*Thank you for bringing us together to share this meal.
Help us to use our time together to celebrate You and bring
glory to Your Kingdom. May this food be a blessing to our
bodies and our bodies to your service. Amen.*

Delicious Green Beans

This recipe was given to me by one of my Rah Rah girls, Jamie Wright. We are both educators, work in the preschool division at church and love to cook. She is a go-getter and can organize any type of event with her eyes closed. She coordinated my daughter's wedding and I didn't worry about a single thing—this mama was a happy camper.

This dish will quickly become a favorite for any family dinner or holiday spread. It's super easy and delicious.

Ingredients

4 cans green beans, drain beans and put in 9 x 13 dish
1 onion, chopped
6 T. butter
1/3 cup brown sugar
1/2 tsp. salt
1/2 tsp. pepper
1 tsp. Worcestershire sauce
Bacon or bacon bits

Directions

1. Chop onion and sprinkle over beans.
2. Combine butter, brown sugar, salt, pepper, and Worcestershire sauce in a sauce pan and cook until bubbly.
3. Pour sauce over beans and onions.
4. Bake at 350 degrees for 20 to 30 minutes
5. Fry 2 to 3 strips of bacon and crumble or use bacon bits and sprinkle over green beans the last 10 minutes of cooking time.

Serves: 8

Poppyseed Bread

Oh my goodness, I've been baking this sweet bread for almost 25 years. I found this recipe in a HomeLife Magazine that I picked up from our church when my daughter was a little girl. The recipe makes five mini loaves—perfect for gift-giving anytime.

The glaze provides a sweet, citrus flavor and it's super moist. I've baked a ton of this bread over the years.

Bread Ingredients

3 cups all-purpose flour
1 1/2 tsp. baking powder
1 1/2 tsp. salt
2 1/4 cups sugar
3 eggs
1 1/2 cups milk
1 1/2 cups oil
1 1/2 Tbsp. poppy seeds
2 tsp. vanilla
2 tsp. butter flavoring

Directions

1. Preheat oven to 350 degrees.
2. Mix together all ingredients. Beat two minutes. Grease and flour 5 mini loaf pans.
3. Fill pans half full with batter.
4. Bake for 1 hour

(continue next page)

Glaze for Bread

3/4 cups sugar
1/4 cup orange juice
1 1/2 tsp. vanilla
1/2 tsp. butter flavoring

Directions

Mix together and pour over hot bread. Let stand 30 minutes. Remove bread from pan.

Day 22
Make the Connection

"They are new every morning; great is your faithfulness."

Lamentations 3:23 NIV

Often we forget to give God the credit for all that we have and all that we are. As Christians, we need to acknowledge that God is good, all the time. He gives us all things and He creates all things.

God created each one of us to know Him, love Him, and to have fellowship with Him. He longs for me to bring my prayers and petitions to Him. And, I feel blessed and thankful that He loves me despite my imperfections.

Some of my favorite moments of the day are spent in prayer. Some of those prayers take place in my car on the way to and from work. I am tucked away in a quiet place and I relish in the conversations I have with Him. Thanking God for His blessings is one way to express my deep and abiding love for Him. I try to make sure my thank you's precede laying out all the things I need from Him.

The Bible tells me that trusting in God's faithfulness each day will make me more confident in His promises and truths. His steadfast love and mercy are greater than any sin I could bring to Him and I am reassured that I can pour out every problem and worry to Him and let Him take it.

What can you do to more deeply connect God to your life? What changes do you need to make?

_____

_____

_____

_____

_____

_____

Point of Focus

"Giving God thanks each day connects my life to His presence."

Scripture Reading

James 1:17

_____

_____

_____

John 11:41

_____

_____

_____

Today, I am thankful for

_____

_____

Prayer

Lord, I want to thank You for all that is good in my life. I am comforted to have You right here in my heart, leading me and guiding me along the way. I am forever blessed to have my quiet time with You, and thank you for the connectedness we share, just as a father to a daughter. I'm thankful for Your veil of protection and pray that I always remember to tell You how grateful I am for the many blessings You have given me. Amen.

Day 23

Be Grateful for Everything

"For everything God created is good, and nothing is to be rejected if it is received with thanksgiving."

1 Timothy 4:4 NIV

Just think about this for a minute. What would your life look like and feel like if you were grateful for every single thing? Sounds impossible doesn't it?

But we know if we commit to praying for a heart of gratitude and thankfulness we will see changes. And we know that we can not be *discontented* and *thankful* at the same time. So if our grateful minds are constantly fixed upon the best, then things become the best, because our Heavenly Father is the BEST.

Write down how you have prayed for a heart of gratitude and the changes you have experienced.

_____

_____

_____

_____

_____

_____

Point of Focus

"A thankful heart prevents a discontented spirit."

Scripture Reading

Psalm 9:1

_____

_____

_____

1 Corinthians 1:4-5

_____

_____

_____

Today, I am thankful for

_____

_____

Prayer

Dear God, thank you for the many blessings You have given me. May I always be reminded of the good in my life—for my family, for the countless times You provided for me in a time of need, and for the kindness that so many others have heaped upon me. Thank you for walking with me through deep waters; for the wisdom to make the best choices, and for restoring me when I am less than I should be. Amen.

Day 24

Let Us All Give Thanks

"I will praise God's name in song and glorify Him with thanksgiving."

Psalm 69:30 NIV

As we approach this day let us take a moment to thank God for what He has done for us.

Let us reflect on the fruit of the spirit: love, joy, peace, patience, kindness, goodness, faithfulness, gentleness and self-control. Let us be thankful for spiritual growth and our salvation in Christ Jesus.

We can prepare for each and every day by turning our eyes upon Him and thank Him for every single blessing we have. He is the provider of all and our gratitude comes from Him exclusively.

The foundation of thanksgiving is found in God's word over and over. Many of the Psalms are a hymnbook filled with praise and worship.

I write notes in my Bible and appreciate when I come across the reminders in the margins where I have included important key points. For example, I wrote that Psalm 91-100 are for thanksgiving. Psalm 135 tells us to praise the Lord, for the Lord is good. And next to Psalm 136 I wrote this is the never-ending story of God's love—He deserves our praise because His words never fail.

Thank God today for all that you have, but most especially for your spiritual possessions, because they are priceless.

Point of Focus

"God deserves all my thanksgiving."

Scripture Reading

Psalm 95:6-7

_____

_____

_____

Psalm 103:20-22

_____

_____

_____

Deuteronomy 8:7-11

_____

_____

_____

Today, I am thankful for

_____

_____

Prayer

Dear Lord, thank you for this beautiful time. Thank you for the gift of gratitude, for Your grace and blessings, and for Your provision, strength, and unconditional love. I will shout with joy and worship You with gladness. I will acknowledge Your greatness, give thanks to You, and bless Your Holy name. May I continue to honor You with my heart of gratitude and freely share with others during each season of thanksgiving. Amen.

Turning What We Have into Enough

"I am not saying this because I am in need, for I have learned to be content whatever the circumstances. I know what it is to be in need, and I know what it is to have plenty. I have learned the secret of being content in any and every situation, whether well fed or hungry, whether living in plenty or in want."

Philippians 4:11-12 NIV

One of my favorite quotes by author, Melody Beattie, says,

"Gratitude unlocks the fullness of life. It turns what we have into enough, and more. It turns denial into acceptance, chaos to order, confusion to clarity. It can turn a meal into a feast, a house into a home, a stranger into a friend."

God's word gives me firm ground to walk on. When I am scared, He gives me strength and courage. When I doubt my abilities, He speaks words of truth. When I become overwhelmed, He instructs me to run to Him and His Word. When I need protection He provides me with a safe haven. It is during my search for peace and contentment that I see everything I need is found in Him.

I am constantly reminded of what He does for me. It is through His love for me that I have more than I ever thought possible.

Point of Focus

"We are to be thankful and count our blessings for what we have, rather than what we want."

Scripture Reading

Psalm 106:1

_____

_____

_____

John 10:10

_____

_____

_____

Job 36:11

_____

_____

_____

Make a list of times when you expressed gratitude and found yourself the beneficiary of more than you expected?

_____

_____

_____

Today, I am thankful for

_____

_____

Prayer

Lord, thank you for Your provision. For knowing what I need and when I
need it. I pray for contentment in every situation and rest in knowing that
what You have for me is more than I could have ever dreamed possible,
and more than I deserve. I am thankful for Your love. In Your Name. Amen.

Day 26

Uncover the Unexpected Moments

"May the LORD now show you kindness and faithfulness, and I too will show you the same favor because you have done this."

2 Samuel 2:6 NIV

Find small miracles of gratitude each day. A bright spot might include an encouraging note sent by a co-worker or friend, or much needed support during a meeting or presentation. Or maybe you were running late and avoided a trouble spot along the way. Whatever it is, there are numerous examples of gratitude and thankfulness in our day, if we look for them.

Reality reminds us that every day won't go as planned and our perfectionist side needs to be totally okay with that. Sometimes juggling all of the responsibilities we are tasked with gets frustrating, but we can look at things in one of two ways—the glass is either half full or the glass is half empty.

You choose. Personally, I'm going with the half full deal. That's what I call moving from a negative to a positive. Remember, there is no need to sweat the small stuff. Instead, make a habit of looking for pockets of gratitude in each day.

Point of Focus

"Small miracles are tucked inside every day."

Scripture Reading

1 Thessalonians 5:18

_____

_____

_____

1 Chronicles 16:34

_____

_____

_____

What are ways you show your gratitude and thankfulness?

_____

_____

_____

Today, I am thankful for

_____

_____

Prayer

Heavenly Father, thank you for all the love and care you give me. Help me to not be overwhelmed, but instead to take each day one step at a time. I am grateful for the friends and family who brighten my day with their kind words and actions. May I always see the goodness You offer me and share love, joy, and kindness with those around me. Amen.

Day 27
Spread Your Attitude of Gratitude

"Wealth and honor come from You; You are the ruler of all things. In Your hands are strength and power to exalt and give strength to all. Now, our God, we Give You Thanks and praise Your glorious name."

1 Chronicles 29:12-13 NIV

Be the one who embraces an attitude of gratitude and share it with those around you. Show friends, family and co-workers they are appreciated.

There are people every day who honor others through a random act of kindness. Maybe it is in the drive-thru line at a local fast food restaurant. There is nothing more surprising and affirming then driving up to the window to find out that a total stranger paid for your order. I guarantee this small action will bring a big smile to your face. If you want to keep the smiles going, then treat the person behind you.

Jesus is the perfect example for generous giving. Through sacrifice and generosity God gave up His Son for us. He didn't just give us a little sampling of this gift; He gave us the entire gift. Over and over again we can look at the love of God and show that same kind of love to all people, everywhere.

Look for ways to spread joy and gratitude. Check on a sick friend, run an errand for a neighbor, or share food from your garden with another family. Just remember it is better to give than receive and every single day presents the perfect opportunity to provide for others. A fringe benefit is you receive the blessing too. Make the spirit of giving contagious.

Point of Focus

"Take action. Doing for others makes the heart happy.
Whatever you do, it will make a difference."

Scripture Reading

Deuteronomy 6:1-12

_____

_____

_____

_____

_____

_____

_____

_____

_____

_____

_____

_____

Today, I am thankful for

_____

_____

Prayer

Dear God, Your generosity abounds as I have been the receiver of Your gifts over and over again. Please teach me to give unselfishly and to be a good steward of the resources you provide. Help me to be generous in my giving and share with others as You have so lovingly done for me. Amen.

Day 28
Be Thankful Through Every Season

"Enter His gates with thanksgiving and His courts with praise.
Give thanks to Him and praise His name."
Psalm 100:4 NIV

The book of Psalms is a beautiful collection of songs and prayers that expresses the heart and soul of mankind. Time and time again we can turn to this book for words of comfort, to seek His direction and wisdom, and to shower Him with praise and worship.

David wrote approximately 73 of the Psalms, while Asaph, Solomon and others contributed to the book. Each of these writers conveyed their thoughts and deep emotions to God, expressing their true feelings that ran the gamut from powerful, to emotional, to life-changing, and to gratefulness. They laid out their hearts before the Lord, signifying the depth of their relationship with Him.

God's desire is for each one of us to have a deep and meaningful relationship with Him that is filled with abundant joy, and a love that stretches far beyond what we can comprehend.

We have the opportunity to reach deep into the depths of our soul to proclaim He is Lord. Psalm 100 is a favorite passage because it says that I can *'shout for joy to the Lord,'* all the while pouring out all the love and appreciation I have for Him with a loving and thankful heart.

Another way I show my love and gratitude to God is by singing praise and worship songs. The songs put a smile on my face and remind me that I have entered joyfully into God's presence. And, I don't just sing the notes— I meditate on the words because they are His truths and promises. I can stand firm in His Word and praise Him for who He is and what He has done for me.

How do you praise God on a daily basis? Write some of your praises here.

_____

_____

_____

_____

_____

_____

_____

_____

_____

_____

_____

Point of Focus

"Being thankful in every season allows me to keep pouring
my love upon the Father."

Scripture Reading

Psalm 35:18

Psalm 50:14

Psalm 34:1-7

Today, I am thankful for

Prayer

Dear Heavenly Father, please let my heart of gratitude honor You and draw others closer to You. You are the reason and source of all that I have and all that I am. I want my attitude of gratitude to be contagious and a light for your Kingdom. I praise Your Holy name, day in and day out, and I dedicate this season of thanksgiving to the King of Kings and give you praise, glory and honor. Amen!

Food for Thought

Dear Gracious Lord,

*I come to you today with arms open wide and
praising You for every person at this table.
Thank you for the daily comforts You so lovingly provide
and for the food that we are about to eat.
May it be nourishing to our souls. Amen.*

Granny's Meatloaf

My maternal grandmother, Vera Tommie Cowart, could cook like nobody's business and she was pleased as punch to serve her family a delicious meal. One of my favorite dishes growing up was her meat loaf. My mother, Amelia Rowland, continued the tradition and is the only family member I know who can recreate this recipe perfectly. When I prepare this dish I get close to the original, but it's not my Granny's or my mother's. And to meet their southern standards, I always serve it with homemade mashed potatoes and purple hull peas with okra and cornbread.

Ingredients

1 lb. ground round meat
1 green bell pepper
1 medium, mild onion
1 egg
1 can chopped tomatoes
1 small can tomato juice
1 sleeve of saltine crackers
Salt and Pepper

Directions

1. Preheat oven to 350 degrees.
2. Using a 8x8 casserole dish and lightly spray cooking spray on bottom and sides of dish.
3. Finely chop bell pepper and onion.
4. Mix ground meat with egg, can tomatoes, tomato juice, bell pepper, and onion, salt, and pepper to taste.
5. Add crushed crackers and mix well.
6. Pour into casserole dish. Add 1/4 cup water around edges.
7. Bake for 1 hour. Check for doneness. Serves 6

Broccoli Cornbread

This is another one of those 'keeper' recipes from my mother-in-law. She was a wonderful cook and weekend lunches were a family favorite. She lived in Shreveport, Louisiana—just an hour from our East Texas home, so it was easy to drive over for a visit and a meal. Some of our best conversations were around the dinner table, filled with family.

She gave me this delicious recipe in March, 1990, and it has been a family favorite ever since. It is delicious and moist.

This dish is super easy to assemble and the left overs freeze well. You can bake in a muffin tin if you desire.

Ingredients

4 eggs, beaten
1 small onion, chopped
1 - 12 oz. carton cottage cheese
1 - 10 1/2 oz. box/bag frozen chopped broccoli, thawed and drained
2 pkgs. Jiffy Cornbread mix
1 1/2 sticks melted margarine

Directions

1. Preheat oven to 350 degrees.
2. Using a 9x13 casserole dish, lightly grease or spray cooking spray on bottom and sides of dish.
3. Mix all ingredients well and pour into the prepared baking dish.
4. Bake for about an hour—it will be lightly browned on top.
5. Cut into squares and serve.

Gratitude that Lasts a Lifetime

*"Let your roots grow down into Him, and let your lives be built on Him.
Then your faith will grow strong in the truth you were taught,
and you will overflow with thankfulness."*

Colossians 2:7 NLT

During this journey we have prayed daily for God to cultivate in us a heart of gratitude. Do you see the difference in your life? I hope your heart has grown in praise and thanksgiving. If giving thanks and expressing our gratitude is truly a part of who we are, then living a life of gratitude is not an option. The gratitude we have been praying for lasts a lifetime.

We will always be faced with a variety of situations and while God doesn't expect us to thank Him for the problems, we should thank Him for His watchful eye and His sovereign ways to help us in our spiritual growth when handling adversity.

To live a life of gratitude is a growing process, and what He wants most is for us to turn to Him every step of the way. This is called 'walking in faith.'

Start a list titled, 'Gratitude Counts' and make note of who you need to take care of in the gratitude department. Don't let too much time pass without thanking others for caring about you.

Point of Focus

"Gratitude is the story we never stop writing."

Colossians 2:6

_____

_____

_____

Ephesians 1:16

_____

_____

_____

1 Chronicles 23:30

_____

_____

_____

Today, I am thankful for

_____

_____

Prayer

Dear Lord, I want to thank you for cultivating a heart of gratitude in me. Teach me to thank others and to encourage them often so I don't lose my way in this journey. I pray that I honor You with my attitude of thankfulness and share it gratefully with You and those around me. Thank you for your provision and protection. I pray these things in Your name. Amen.

Day 30

Goals for Life

*"Yes, you will be enriched in every way so that you can always be generous.
And when we take your gifts to those who need them,
they will thank God."*

2 Corinthians 9:11 NLT

This study concludes with us walking in 30 days of thankfulness and gratitude.

But the deeper, more meaningful part of the challenge is for us to cultivate a heart full of gratitude that will stay with us long after this study is complete.

The challenge is to encourage you to give thanks and praise to the King of Kings, and to look deep into your soul to find what could be accomplished through a genuine, caring, and gracious heart.

I hope each of you has experienced life-changing purpose as you pursue your passion for a grateful lifestyle that only comes from your persistence to live in Christ.

Take time today to develop gratitude goals and write each one down. What do you want to accomplish as you grow in gratitude during this next year? How can you practice daily thankfulness?

_____

_____

_____

Point of Focus

"Gratitude is a goal that should never end."

Scripture Reading

Hebrews 13:8

_____

_____

_____

Galatians 1:3

_____

_____

_____

Ephesians 4:6

_____

_____

_____

Today, I am thankful for

Prayer

Dear Lord, I want to thank you for cultivating a heart of gratitude in me. Teach me to appreciate others and to encourage them every chance I get. May I honor You with heartfelt thanks and share it gratefully with those around me. I pray that my commitment to live as Christ lives will shine bright in my actions and love for others. I pray the goals I set before You are Your Will and direction for my life, and not of selfish desire to accomplish on my own. I pray these things in Your Name, Amen.

To commemorate the 30 day 'Thankful Heart' study, write a prayer that expresses your heart's desires to please God. Thank Him for all that He does through you, and in you. His grace makes it possible for us to abound in thanksgiving--every day of the year.

_____

_____

_____

_____

_____

_____

_____

_____

_____

_____

_____

_____

_____

Food for Thought

God is great, God is good,
Let us thank Him for our food;
By His hand we must be fed,
Give us Lord, our daily bread. Amen.

Confetti Cheese Ball

My sister, Robin Conway, always makes this fabulous cheese ball as an appetizer to our pre-holiday meals. In other words, we graze around a snack table while we are finishing up the main entree' and this recipe is the ticket. She shared it with me a few years ago and it became an immediate favorite. It's that good. So, when we're together, I always insist she bring the cheese ball. Oh, as a side note, the cheese ball is rolled in crushed up corn/tortilla chips, and during the holiday season we roll it in red/green chips for a festive look.

Ingredients

2 - 8 oz. cream cheese, softened
1 package/jar of dried beef, chopped
4 green onion, chopped with stems included
1/4 tsp. garlic powder
1/2 tsp. Liquid Smoke
1/4 tsp. Worcestershire sauce
2 handfuls corn/tortilla chips
Crackers to serve

Directions

1. In a medium bowl, combine together the cream cheese, beef, onion, garlic powder, Liquid Smoke, and Worcestershire sauce.
2. Form into a ball and refrigerate for about 30 minutes.
3. Crush corn/tortilla chips in a large ziploc bag. Placed the chilled cheese ball in the bag of crushed chips and roll to coat.
4. Place ball on a decorative or festive plate and serve with crackers.
Serves: 8-10

Fiesta Chicken

This recipe is a shared favorite of both my mother and mother-in-law. It's easy, bakes in one dish and is a great comfort food. There are many varieties of this recipe available, but this is my go-to favorite. You could add taco seasoning for a flavor variation and call it Mexican Chicken.

This dish is perfect for the fall season when the nights are cooler and it's a great entree' for a group.

Ingredients

1 can Cream of Chicken Soup
1/2 cup water
3/4 cup uncooked long grain rice
1 1/2 cups of Salsa (I use Mild Pace Picante)
1 can of whole kernel corn (you can also 1 cup of frozen whole kernel corn)
2 large chicken breasts cut in pieces
1 cup of shredded cheese (I like the Fiesta Cheese blend)
Paprika

Directions

1. Heat the oven to 375 degrees.
2. In a large bowl, stir the soup, salsa, water, corn and rice and pour into a greased 9x13 dish.
3. Top with chicken pieces.
4. Sprinkle with paprika and cover with foil.
5. Bake for 50 minutes or until the chicken is cooked through and the rice is tender.
6. Remove from oven and sprinkle with cheese. Let stand until the cheese is melted.   Serves: 6-8

Epilogue

Thank you for reading 'A Thankful Heart: 30 Days to the Grateful Life.' I pray you were blessed by this study.

Each day's message was written to help us understand about the never ending season of thanksgiving that we are offered. It is about seeking out the big and little blessings in our day-to-day lives—looking for ALL of the goodness that our loving God provides.

It is my commitment to being a 'Jesus Girl' that brings me pure joy and a relationship with my Heavenly Father that goes beyond what I could have ever imagined. This book is one way for me thank Him. I want these words to bring Him glory.

I have realized over the course of my life that it is God, first and foremost, who loves me unconditionally and provides me with the protection and provision I so need. Everything I am and everything I have is because of Him.

In return, I want to thank Him with all of the gratitude I can muster up. No matter what comes my way, I owe Him my life—this is my testimony and I am thankful for the experiences.

Bless you as you continue on this daily journey of cultivating a grateful heart.

Acknowledgements

When I started this journey three years ago, the goal was to write a women's devotional book. But God. He had other ideas. A few months later I sensed God nudging me to launch a blog. And, so I did. With the encouragement and assistance of my friends and resident tech guys, Scott Floyd and Michael Gras, things were up and running quickly. I am so thankful for their expertise and patience to help me navigate every step.

Thank you to a special group of precious friends and sisters of faith, (Robin, Gail, Betsy, Jamie, Dana, Claire, Jennifer, Michelle, Jo Anna, Suzanne and Melanie) whom I call my Rah-Rah girls for giving me the courage to move forward. They were willing to walk this journey even when they were not sure what this journey was all about. They have read and edited countless blog posts, created images and calendars, and submitted ideas and storylines to keep the content fresh. Their laughter, prayers, and encouragement have been huge and I am forever grateful.

This book is a reality because of my friend, Kim Stewart, who gave me a big push and said, "get this study out there girl." Many thanks. To Leigh Ellen Eades for your prayers, proofreading, and attention to detail that added so much to this study. You are a breath of fresh air.

To Jana Kennedy-Spicer, Kristine Brown, Alisa Nicaud, Sue Moore Donaldson, and Stephanie K. Adams for giving me opportunities to write, for sharing my content, for teaching me cool tips and tricks along the way, and for telling me I could do this. I am forever blessed by your friendships.

And to Megan Hawkins Lawson, my former student and forever friend, thank you for using your God given talent to create beautiful artwork as part of the free resources available for this study.

Connect with the Author

Do you have a beloved family recipe of your own? Mitzi would love for you to send her a copy at peacefullyimperfect@gmail.com. Who knows, your recipe just might appear in her next book.

Because Mitzi loves interacting with her community of PI friends, here is your invitation to join her on several platforms.

Website

www.peacefullyimperfect.net

Twitter

@a_joyfulpeace

Facebook

https://www.facebook.com/peacefullyimperfect1/

Pinterest

https://www.pinterest.com/mrneely2/

Instagram

https://www.instagram.com/mitzi4936/

Complimentary Resources

The following free gifts are available under *Resources* at:
www.peacefullyimperfect.net

30 Day Calendar

Scripture Artwork

30 Day Scripture Reading Plan

Scripture Cards

Made in the USA
Lexington, KY
19 November 2019

57268844R00074